insight text guide

Sabrina Chakman

Elie Wiesel

First published in 2001. Reprinted 2009, 2011, 2012, 2013, 2015. Revised and updated based on Marion Wiesel's 2006 translation of *Night*; reprinted in 2016, 2017 (twice), 2019, 2020, 2021, 2022, 2023, 2024, 2025.

Insight Publications Pty Ltd
3/350 Charman Road
Cheltenham VIC 3192
Australia
Tel: +61 3 8571 4950
Email: books@insightpublications.com.au

www.insightpublications.com.au

National Library of Australia Cataloguing-in-Publications entry:

Chakman, Sabrina
Ellie Wiesel's Night: insight text guide / Sabrina Chakman.
9781875882489 (pbk.)
843.914

Other ISBNs:
9781925175158 (digital)

Cover design: The Modern Art Production Group

Proudly Printed in Australia by Ligare Book Printers

contents

CHARACTER MAP

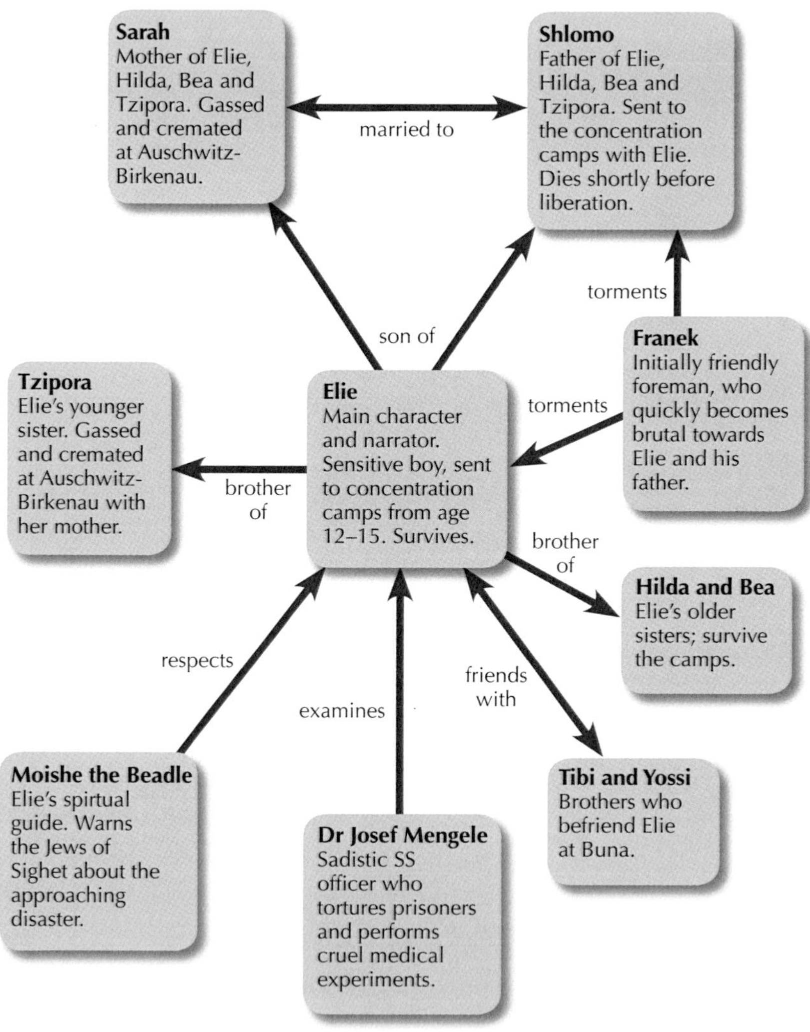

INTRODUCTION

It was an interview with François Mauriac, the famous French Catholic writer (who wrote the foreword to *Night*), that inspired Elie Wiesel to tell the story of the horror he suffered and witnessed as a teenager in the infamous Nazi concentration camps. A fairly typical response to trauma is that people do not want to talk about their experiences. Wiesel was one of them, but he was helped to see that he could work for the benefit of humanity in writing his autobiography. Wiesel is now a famous and tireless advocate for human rights and a university professor who has established the Elie Wiesel Foundation for Humanity. He has written more than forty books and has won numerous awards for his work for human rights.

Important dates in Wiesel's life

1928 – Born 30 September in Sighet, Romania (pre-war Hungary). Note: Wiesel says that Sighet is a 'little town in Transylvania'; the book cover refers to it as Hungary but in the blurb about the author it is in Romania. The Hungarian police have jurisdiction over Sighet rather than the Romanian police as you might expect. The explanation for this apparent confusion is that Transylvania is a region of Romania; Romania belonged to Hungary until 1947.

1944 – Deported by the Nazis to Birkenau and Auschwitz, then transported to Buchenwald.

1945 – Father dies in Buchenwald, 28 January.

1945 – Elie liberated from the camp,11 April. Lives in French orphanage.

1948 – Begins study at the Sorbonne in Paris.

1954 – Decides to tell his story after interview with François Mauriac.

1958 – *Night* published.

1963 – Becomes a citizen of the USA.

1972 – Serves as Distinguished Professor of Judaic Studies at City University, New York.

1976 – Becomes the Andrew W. Mellon Professor in the Humanities at Boston University.

1978 – Appointed chairman of the President's Commission on the Holocaust by US President Carter.

1980 – Becomes the Founding Chairman of the USA Holocaust Memorial Council.

1986 – Wins Nobel Prize for Peace and subsequently establishes the Elie Wiesel Foundation for Humanity.

CONTEXT & BACKGROUND

Adolf Hitler (1889–1945)

Born in Austria, Hitler became the leader of a fanatically nationalistic (and racist) political party called the National Socialist German Workers' Party (Nazi Party) soon after the end of World War I in which he served. In 1923 he led a group of ex-servicemen and thugs in an attempt to overthrow the government of Bavaria (a state in Germany) for which he was imprisoned. In gaol he wrote *Mein Kampf (My Battle/Struggle)* which expressed his philosophy of so-called 'Aryan' superiority and Jewish inferiority; the hallmark of his regime was his passionate anti-Semitism. Through political intrigue and blackmail, Hitler became the chancellor of Germany in 1933, and rapidly dismantled the democratic structures, turning Germany into a totalitarian state. In 1934 he appointed himself the *Führer* (supreme leader) of the so-called 'Third Reich' (Third Empire) which he believed would last a thousand years! He re-occupied the Rhineland in 1936, annexed (incorporated into Germany) Austria and Czechoslovakia in 1938, and invaded Poland in 1939. This last led to the declaration of war (World War II: 1939–45) by the Allies. During his period in power, Hitler ordered the establishment of concentration camps expressly for the extermination of Jews and other ethnic and political groups he called subhuman or enemies of Nazism. In 1945, with Germany close to surrender, Hitler committed suicide, thus avoiding capture and trial by the Allied forces.

Nazism in Germany

Hitler founded the Nazi party in 1921 with just a few hundred members. The economic depression in Germany after the World War I (1914–18) particularly during the 1920s and 1930s, and Hitler's personal charisma, led to the rapid growth of its membership. Although the Nazis never won an absolute majority of the vote in a democratic election, in July 1932 they won more votes than any other party in Germany.

In 1933 the Nazis declared a national boycott of all Jewish-owned shops. Jews who did not wear the yellow star were subject to execution.

In 1935 Hitler escalated his anti-Jewish policies: the Nuremberg Laws deprived Jews of German citizenship, and sexual relations and marriages between Jews and non-Jews were declared illegal. Later it became illegal for non-Jews to work for Jews and for Jews to study with non-Jews. Jews were also banned from a number of professions.

On 10 November 1938, discriminatory policy changed to wholesale violence in a pogrom which has become known as *Kristallnacht* – the night of the broken glass. The windows of almost every synagogue and of Jewish businesses were shattered; 91 Jews were murdered and 30,000 were arrested and sent to concentration camps where many died.

How Hitler isolated the Jews

One of Hitler's tactics was to establish ghettos using the SS to round up Jews, forcing them to leave their homes and crowd together in the poorest part of their towns. They were required to relinquish valuables, they were subject to curfews, and they lost their independence and social standing. Jews in high profile jobs, for example in the government and universities, were dismissed without warning. The yellow star they were forced to wear at all times made them easy targets for the Germans.

Jewish history

Jews have lived in Europe for at least two thousand years and by World War II they were very much part of German society. However, an examination of Jewish history tells us this was not the first time they had been turned against by friends and neighbours.

The Jews originated from nomadic Semitic tribes who lived in the Middle East and have a known history that goes back probably 4000 years. The Old Testament of the Bible is really a history of these early Jews and includes the story of Abraham who converted his tribe to the belief of a monotheistic God (a belief that there is only one god) at a time in history when people worshipped many gods often in the form of objects or animals. Later, according to the Old Testament, the Jews were forced to flee Egypt, where many had settled, to escape the persecution that resulted from holding different religious beliefs from the rest of the population.

In the last 2000 years, Jews have lived all over the Middle East and throughout Europe, and have suffered ongoing persecution. For example, in 170 BC in Syria, under a Greek ruler, Jews were massacred for refusing to worship Greek gods. In 1290, Jews were expelled from England because they were said, wrongly, to perform ritual murder. In 1394, all Jews were expelled from France. In 1492, Spanish Jews were massacred or driven out. In Russia, Jews were massacred in pogroms throughout the nineteenth century.

Jewish identity

The question of whether Jews are a race, a religion or a culture has no simple answer. Jews identify themselves as being Jewish even if they are not religious, and Jews come from many different countries. The answer to what being Jewish really means is probably a mix of all of the above.

For more detail read *The Complete Idiot's Guide to Jewish History and Culture* by Rabbi Benjamin Blech. Don't be offended by the title – the author is conforming to the other titles used in a series of books, which are usually computer manuals, such as *The Complete Idiot's Guide to Networking Your Home*. The style of the books is humorous and the author assumes no prior knowledge. He leads readers through information in a user-friendly, but not condescending, fashion.

Jewish religion and Holydays

Judaism is based on the study of the Torah and the Talmud. Family is central to religious life and religious observance is expressed through High Holyday festivals, often culminating in feasts and celebrations. In *Night*, Wiesel mentions:

- *Shabbat*, the Sabbath, which begins on Friday evening with the appearance of the first star in the sky and ends on Saturday evening. Jews are not supposed to work on the Sabbath, which in modern times includes driving a car and turning on power.

- *Pesach* (Passover), which commemorates the escape of the Jews from slavery in Egypt.
- *Rosh Hashanah*, the Jewish New Year (the Hebrew calendar differs from the Christian one).
- *Yom Kippur*, which is the Day of Atonement when Jews ask for God's forgiveness of their sins.

Jewish practices

- *Kashrut* – Jews are required to observe dietary laws, called kashrut, which include keeping meat and milk separate.
- *Kosher* – Food is kosher if it is prepared according to practices based on laws regarding food preparation (*kashrut*) that are in the Torah. This includes a way of slaughtering animals for meat that follows a prescribed procedure which is considered to be more humane.

Adolf Hitler and the 'Final Solution'

WWII began on 3 September 1939, following the rise of the Nazi Party and Hitler's drive to take over Europe to create what he called the 'Third Reich', which was to be a new era led by Germany. Hitler's plan to exterminate the Jews of Europe, as well as other 'undesirables' or opponents, was what he euphemistically called the 'Final Solution' (to the Jewish question).

He used the well-established pattern of anti-Jewish sentiment (this became anti-Semitism on racial, rather than strictly religious, grounds) to gather support for his idea that Germans (whom he termed 'Aryans') were the Master Race. Aryans were, in fact, never the blue-eyed, blond Germans as the Nazis claimed. Historians believe they were probably an ancient people who spread from what is now Iran and Iraq, across the region from India through to Eastern Europe. Nevertheless, Hitler believed he should cleanse the world of 'inferior' groups. He attributed Germany's economic and political troubles, including Communism which he labelled a Jewish conspiracy, to the Jews. He masterminded heinous (abominable) procedures to carry out his 'final solution'.

Why didn't Jews flee?

In *Night*, we see the Jewish people responding to the news of threats to their wellbeing in ways that may seem strange to us. The question of why they did not immediately pack up and flee their homes is often raised. The answer, in part, lies in the history of persecution that the Jews have suffered from the time they chose to be monotheistic (believing in one God). The experience of being outsiders and suffering persecution was a recurring one. The tragedy of what happened in Nazi Germany was that, for a time, Jews had felt quite secure and had, perhaps, dropped their guard.

It can also be argued that Jews were very reluctant to move away from established centres because of the close nature of their community involvement and worship, which relied on access to a synagogue and services, such as kosher food. Another problem was the difficulty of finding somewhere to go. Many Jews did try to leave Germany and the other occupied countries prior to and during the war. However most countries, including Australia, closed their doors, letting only a small number of people in (often only children) even after their governments knew of the death camps.

One of the reasons that Elie's father and many of the Jews in his town did not believe the warnings of Moishe the Beadle was that Germany was such a cultured and civilised country. Many Jews were so assimilated that they considered themselves German before anything else, even before their Jewish identity. They simply could not believe that the mad acts of brutality and hatred that occurred during Hitler's regime could come from their neighbours and friends.

There are several references in *Night* to the Jews' disbelief of the stories they heard about the Holocaust. They did not believe those things could happen 'in the middle of the twentieth century!' (p.8), despite the events in Germany. Elie's father says he is too old to pack up and start again in a new country; others can't believe the Germans could be so cruel. Some Jews doubted Hitler's ability to wipe out a whole people who were scattered all over Europe – there seemed to be a desire to believe only the best about people. Perhaps it was a collective exhaustion and a group refusal to countenance history repeating itself.

Concentration camps and the Holocaust

The most terrible of Hitler's strategies to 'purify' Germany was the use of concentration camps from 1933 to 1945 in Germany and other European countries to imprison political and ideological opponents. At the concentration camps, millions of Jews were murdered, along with so-called enemies of the Nazi regime, Soviet prisoners of war and people deemed inferior, such as gypsies, homosexuals, the ill and the disabled. Romanian Jews, such as Elie Wiesel and the Jews in Sighet, were not affected until towards the end of the war because Romania was a German ally and only occupied by the Germans later in the war.

Auschwitz-Birkenau, possibly the most terrible of the concentration camps, was one that Elie Wiesel survived. This was in fact a vast camp complex that held prisoners and forced people into slave labour. It included gas chambers and other means of extermination. Over four million individuals died there between 1941 and 1944 under horrific circumstances.

After 1945, many camp officials were tried for their war crimes and imprisoned or executed. Today, Auschwitz, in Poland, remains open as a museum and memorial to victims of the Holocaust.

Dr Josef Mengele

The chief physician at Auschwitz, Dr Josef Mengele was one of several doctors who met the trainloads of Jews arriving at the camp daily. He decided who was to be sent to the gas chambers immediately and who would live a little longer, to be worked to death or to facilitate his inhumane medical experiments. He was a sadist who tortured women and children under the pretext of doing medical science. Any experiment he wished to perform was permitted, no matter how brutal. He was feared and hated by the camp inmates for his cruelty, particularly because he was a medical doctor. He is believed to have drowned in the late 1970s in Brazil, where he lived after evading capture and prosecution by the war crimes tribunal set up after the war.

Elie Wiesel's experiences of the camps

In *Night* Elie Wiesel experiences four different camps.

- *Auschwitz* is the first with its reception centre Birkenau. Elie was then about fifteen years old (p.30). Auschwitz is horrifying: the chimneys billow black smoke produced by burning slaughtered people; the sinister Dr Mengele oversees the selection process; children's bodies are tipped into the open pits of flames; in the floorless barracks the prisoners' feet sink into mud; it is the place Elie calls the 'antechamber of hell' (p.34). Although Elie's first impressions are that Auschwitz is better than Birkenau, this is quickly dispelled when he sees the sign over its entrance, *'Work makes you free'* (p.40). The irony is obvious, and hunger and brutality soon become a reality.
- *Buna* is the second camp (pp.47–84). Here Elie meets the Czech brothers, Tibi and Yossi, and works in the electronics factory which he finds relatively easy although he suffers under the erratic Kapo, Idek, and the foreman, Franek. He and his father are beaten, and Elie is forced to relinquish his gold tooth; he ends up in hospital with an infected foot and fears his leg is amputated. He witnesses the senseless shooting and hanging of prisoners and spends the High Holydays accusing his God of abandoning the Jews. Incongruous military marching music and bells that regulate all the prisoners' activities punctuate his time at Buna. He describes them as being 'terrible days. We received more blows than food. The work was crushing' (p.77).
- *Gleiwitz* is the third camp. Elie decides to leave Buna even though he could have stayed as a patient in the hospital (p.82).They endure a long march to eventually arrive at Gleiwitz where they stay for three days.
- *Buchenwald* is the final camp. After being crowded into cattle wagons, Elie and the surviving prisoners are sent to Buchenwald where the inmates starve because provisions have been withdrawn altogether. Here, Elie's father dies shortly before Elie is liberated.

Propaganda

How do some leaders manage to turn seemingly normal and civilised populations into killers, either actively or by complicity? Psychological texts discuss the effectiveness of propaganda, which is the intense dissemination of very biased material to convince people of a particular point of view. Hitler had a very effective propaganda ministry which controlled the spread of information. The phenomena of mass hysteria and peer pressure also incline people to join with a group and to adopt its views and behaviours, even when they would not normally act in those ways. These elements were part of the Nazi strategy.

Q Research some of Hitler's 'effective propaganda departments' to help you understand the genesis (origins) of the horrors that *Night* depicts.

Key point

The events in Germany and the Holocaust would have seemed familiar to many Jews and may, in part, explain their passive acceptance of their fate. The Torah, the first five books of the Old Testament (in the Bible) of Jewish history and law, which all observant Jews are expected to know well, outlines the pattern of exile, slavery and persecution that has plagued the Jewish people. Many religious Jews believe that they must wait for the Messiah (the great saviour sent by God, prophesied in the Old Testament) before they will be saved and led to the promised land.

Q Reflect on what you have learned about Judaism so far. How does this information explain Elie's determination to stay with his father?

Survivor guilt

Many Jews feel guilt at having survived while so many others, equally innocent, died. The guilt associated with survival itself, not to mention the strategies by which survival was secured, is an issue that continues to haunt many who were involved. Jewish Community Services provides support groups to assist survivors with the issues arising from their war experiences.

Night was not written to make innocent people feel guilty. However, the book does raise the question of 'who is guilty'. Was the world guilty simply by being passive, guilty of complicity by pleading ignorance, or guilty of hiding behind claims that they were just following orders?

Responding to the Holocaust

Elie's story leaves the reader with the feeling that death is not necessarily the worst thing that can happen, yet it is our instinct to avoid it that makes us try to endure unspeakable horrors.

The lessons of the Holocaust can be seen as personal or as universal. Personal lessons raise questions for individuals about their own values and attitudes, about religious faith, about the importance placed on family and community, about the determination to make the most of all situations, and about the steps taken to endure and survive.

Universal lessons raise issues that have plagued humans throughout history and continue to do so, such as racism and xenophobia (fear of strangers or those who are different), violence, war, the power for good and evil of the collective, the abuses of political power, the search for ethical ways to live, the relationship between generations, and relationships between human beings and God.

Q In your view, does *Night* show that death is not necessarily the worst thing that can happen to human beings?

Remembering the Holocaust – is it relevant?

It is often said that, as the events recorded in *Night* happened over fifty years ago, it is time to let them go, to move on, and to stop dredging up the unpleasantness of the past. A common response to this is that we *must* continue to remind ourselves, so that such atrocities will never occur again. To this end, there are many books, exhibitions and activities available.

From time to time, there are exhibitions in Australia about Anne Frank, a Jewish girl who hid with her family in the annex of her father's warehouse with the help of non-Jewish friends. She wrote her now-famous diary before being discovered and sent to her death just before her sixteenth birthday in the Bergen-Belsen concentration camp. The house, in Amsterdam, is preserved as a museum. Many schoolchildren attend these exhibitions and some become very distressed after the visit. Clearly, that is not the intention of taking the children, but it is worth asking how such a reminder of the Holocaust would affect you, even if you are not Jewish. Do you think such exhibitions are a good idea? Remember, in this discussion, that the Holocaust of 1939–1945 was not the last time people abused power and position to inflict war, and even genocide, on innocent populations. Elie Wiesel warns us against becoming complacent or assuming such events will not be repeated.

Q Does *Night* help to persuade you that it is important and relevant to remember the Holocaust?

Comparative Holocausts

There are university and school faculties devoted to the study of comparative holocausts; although the attempted extermination of the Jews during WWII is possibly the worst and most infamous example of genocide, it is certainly not the only one. Currently the term 'ethnic cleansing' is still used by various political regimes and leaders to justify attacks and massacres of people from different ethnic groups. For example, the Serbians 'justified' the killing and displacement of Kosovars on these grounds. This can be compared with Hitler's 'final solution'.

Q Examine what happened in Cambodia under Pol Pot, in Rwanda at the hands of feuding warlords, in Uganda under Idi Amin and in recent times massacres in Yugoslavia, Serbia and East Timor. Consider whether such events and/or any other recent incidents have similar foundations to those that started the Holocaust.

Anti-Semitism and racial discrimination

Consider other events happening in our own backyard. You might consider the controversy surrounding Helen Darville, who wrote *The Hand That Signed The Paper* under the name Helen Demidenko. Darville wrote about the Holocaust using a Ukrainian narrator perceived by some to be anti-Semitic. The book, and the fact that it won the literary establishment's highly valued Miles Franklin Literary Award in 1995, caused heated debate about racism in our society and the necessity for ongoing vigilance. Reflect too on the political and social climate from which the One Nation Party emerged in the late 1990s.

Q Consider the treatment of Australia's Aborigines. When Europeans first settled Australia, they felt it was their right to take the land; some also felt it was their right to wipe out the indigenous people. What was their reasoning? Was it justified?

Freedom of speech and Holocaust denial

The Age carried an article on 29 July 2000 about Norman Finkelstein, an American author who claims that there is a 'Holocaust industry' through which Zionist groups are using the tragedy for profit and to pre-empt criticism of Jews and of the state of Israel. He argues that Elie Wiesel participates in the 'sacralisation of the Holocaust … for his standard fee of $25,000'. Some people accuse Finkelstein of being a monster, a 'self-hating Jew' who has joined the ranks of Holocaust deniers – a charge that Finkelstein vigorously rebuts.

A high-profile Holocaust denier is British historian, David Irving. He and his supporters claim that the Holocaust did not happen as recorded and that the figure of six million deaths in camps such as Auschwitz is grossly exaggerated. Irving has tried to gain entry to Australia to speak publicly, but the government has denied him a visa. You could research Irving's position and learn why he is banned from many countries. Consider those who may be affected by Irving's attitudes and statements.

Q Should freedom of speech be extended to people such as David Irving?

In Australia we pride ourselves on democracy, tolerance and freedom. The One Nation Party became a platform for views that were offensive to some and potentially socially divisive. It is timely to consider just how tolerant and unprejudiced we are as a nation.

Q Is hatred of 'the other' (i.e. outsiders) inevitable? Can democracy respond appropriately to such challenges?

The work of Elie Wiesel and the foundation he heads reminds us of the necessity of constant vigilance against forces that can damage the values we try to uphold. On the Wiesel Foundation website you will find examples of essays that have been written by American college students as submissions in the Elie Wiesel Prize in Ethics. One topic requests a response to facing an ethical dilemma in this complex world.

Q What ethical issues in today's world spring to mind that you could write about?

The aftermath

Many decades after WWII, the world is still grappling to find the appropriate response to the Holocaust. Germany's response has been to institute a system of financial reparation to Jews who lost everything and were incarcerated during the war.

We are faced with ethical questions about the relationship between the perpetrators of war crimes and their victims. An international military tribunal convened the Nuremberg War Trials, held between November 1945 and October 1946, to try to exact some justice for the wrongs committed. Twenty-four prominent Nazis were tried and ten of the twelve sentenced to death were executed by hanging. Hitler and his wife, Eva Braun, committed suicide towards the end of the war.

However, legal victory is cold comfort to those who saw their entire families murdered in a brutal fashion and who lost their homes, their statehood and their lives. In September 2000, an American businessman gained the help of Polish authorities to have the synagogue in the Polish town of Auschwitz reopened. There are no Jews remaining there to use it, but it serves as a reminder of what could have been.

Anti-Semitism is not a thing of the past. In Europe, the neo-Nazi movement which is characterised by skin-heads and the Hitler salute, has a significant following. In Australia, the Council of Christians and Jews was established in 1985 to counteract prejudice and xenophobia in a direct response to the Holocaust and negative teachings about Jews.

Reflect on the attitudes you hear expressed about various ethnic groups. You will find many reasons embedded in negative and discriminatory stereotypes about other ethnic groups that suggest it is worthwhile studying a text such as *Night* in the 21st century.

The 'lessons' of *Night*

The 'lessons' of *Night* stem from the suffering caused by war, bigotry, hatred and the inhumanity of humankind. Such events find their basis in the many reasons that lead people to follow someone like Adolf Hitler: political naivety, innocence, gullibility, ignorance, fear, the need for a leader or saviour, historical circumstances that enable a leader to gain power, the 'charisma' of a powerful leader and so on.

Q As you read and study *Night*, consider what 'lessons' you learn about war, humanity and suffering.

GENRE, STYLE & STRUCTURE

Definitions

The following terms are used in this guide to describe the language in *Night*.

Genre – The category designated for different kinds of writing.

- *Example*: Science fiction and autobiography are genres of writing.

Irony – The use of words to say the opposite of what they normally mean.

- *Example*: When Elie's father says 'So what? It's not lethal …' (p.11), referring to having to wear the yellow star, it is ironic because, indeed, they did die of it, or at least of what it represented.

Imagery and figurative language – Metaphors and similes are used to represent meaning and to suggest a relationship between objects that does not literally exist.

- *Example:* Elie will remember forever the children burnt to death. He sees the bodies of little children 'transformed into smoke under a silent sky' (p.34). In this image the smoke literally rises into the sky from their burnt bodies and the silence suggests that no one, not even God, responds to the tragedy of the massacre. This image has powerful connotations (associated meanings) that embody Elie's distress and the awful reality of the gas chambers.

Motif – A recurring theme, idea, pattern or symbol.

- *Example:* Wiesel uses features of his experience such as fire, heat, cold, snow and bells as motifs to enrich his storytelling. For instance, the extremes of temperature become symbolic of extreme cruelty.

Style – The characteristic manner in which a text is written.

- *Example:* a book may be written in a humorous, factual, poetic or descriptive style.

Structure – The arrangement of the parts of a text or document.

- *Example:* In *Night*, events are arranged in chronological order.

Another common device used in novels and films is flashback, when past events are inserted, often to heighten understanding of present events or a character's behaviour or attitudes.

Symbolism – The use of an object that represents or stands for something else, often an object used to suggest a feeling or concept.

- *Example:* Eyes used as 'the windows to the soul'. In other words, Wiesel describes people's eyes as being bright or dull or dim to indicate their state of mind. Examine the references to Moishe's eyes in pages 3–8. At first, Elie tells us that he 'liked his wide, dreamy eyes' (p.3). Then, after witnessing atrocities in Galicia, 'The joy in his eyes was gone' (p.7) and 'tears, like drops of wax, flowed from his eyes' (p.7). 'He closed his eyes, as if to escape time' (p.7) and, eventually, 'he would drift through synagogue ... eyes cast down ... avoiding people's gaze' (p.8).

Genre – autobiography

Night is an autobiography, a person's written account of their life. In this case, it is Elie Wiesel's vivid account of the time he spent, at about age fifteen, in Hitler's concentration camps of Auschwitz, Buchenwald and Buna. It covers a short but highly significant part of his life, depicting real events and also showing others' responses to the plight of the Jews from Sighet. The book ends with Elie's liberation from Buchenwald, a young man so changed he could not recognise himself. After being liberated, he went to France where he studied at the Sorbonne, in France, and became a journalist.

As autobiography, *Night* is not formal history, but rather a portrayal of a life and time from a limited point of view. It is not a novel because the events and people portrayed really did exist, but the genre gives Wiesel the freedom to use literary devices to enhance and enrich the telling of his story with images, repeated motifs and structural devices which will be discussed in more detail in this guide. Such devices, important in enlivening accounts of actual experiences, add to the readability of the book without detracting from its validity.

An example is Wiesel's use of fire, heat, cold, snow and bells as motifs. These would have been features of his real experience, but in structuring the writing around their repetition, the significance of each is revealed. You will notice that it is often very hot when the Jews are forced to sit and wait outside or are crowded together in cattle trucks. Similarly, it is often freezing when they are forced to march for hours in thin prison clothes and bare feet, or to sleep outside in the snow. The extremes of temperature are symbolic of the extreme cruelty of the situation, as well as being a literal representation of the circumstances.

Point of view – first-person narrator

Night is a first-person narrative, meaning that the writer talks about himself as 'I' and describes events and characters as they appear to him. Wiesel tells his story as an adult looking back on the experiences he endured as a boy of fifteen – the story is told from the point of view of a retrospective narrator.

When the adult writer is referred to in this guide, he is called Wiesel; when he is referred to as the boy in the story, he is called Elie, which is the shortened form of Eliezer.

Key point

This personal account of the horror of life in a concentration camp is told from the point of view of Wiesel as an adult reflecting on his history. This retrospective viewpoint is worth thinking about: the perspective of the author has a considerable effect on how readers respond to the information and descriptions. Although the events described are based in truth, it is fair to say we have only got Elie Wiesel's account here to examine.

Consider the effect of different points of view if this narrative were written:

- as a diary written at the time by someone who was really there, like Anne Frank
- by an outsider who conducted research into the Holocaust and wrote an account

- based on an interview with Wiesel, using his own words but not told by him.

Possible responses to a diary include a more emotional connection because the perspective is from someone living the events and, in Elie Wiesel's case, telling it as a fifteen-year-old. In *Night*, though, the retrospective narrator is an adult and he brings considerable maturity, as well as understanding forged by the experience, to his record.

Readers may find a documentary-style account, based on research, to be very useful in its objectivity, but they may find the human element missing. This can be a positive and a negative.

An interview can appear to be factual and reliable, but we need to be aware that whenever a writer becomes involved, we will necessarily get his or her perspective on the material.

Structure – chronological time

The story is a linear narrative using the structure of chronological time, punctuated with references to passing days, events, seasons and years.

The relatively peaceful years, 1941, 1942 and 1943, are described through references to their most outstanding events such as the retreat of enemies and the domestic concerns of the family, such as finding a husband for Hilda.

The Jewish High Holydays are also used as markers of time, as well as being moments of significance for the Wiesel family. This heightens the sense of loss when Rosh Hashanah and Yom Kippur are celebrated in the camp in a fashion so opposite to what was normal.

Even 1944 is described positively: 'It was a year like so many others, with its spring, its engagements, its weddings, and its births' (p.8).

The time of day and night

The recording of the time of day creates a sense of immediacy in the writing. Importantly, this also highlights the excruciating slowness of time, the tragic consequences of just one night, and the transience of a life – life, there at night, can be extinguished by morning. Wiesel uses the falling of night to create a suitable atmosphere of darkness, a backdrop against which to describe danger and suffering.

The seasons

Likewise, the seasons mark the increasing hardship and desperation of the prisoners' condition. The cold and snow are symbols of the position of the Jews. The early part of *Night* takes place in spring, a time traditionally associated with renewal and optimism. The irony aside, Wiesel records the attitudes of his friends as being consistent with the season. The reader, having started to develop a sense of dread, reads of the wonderful weather at the time of Passover, as though the elements are out of touch with reality and ought to be giving more realistic cues. However, the hot summer sun becomes suitably menacing when the Jews have to sit outside without shelter or water for hours, awaiting their first deportation.

The reader can interpret a deeper meaning than is immediately obvious in the words at the beginning of page 66: 'The summer was coming to an end. The Jewish year was almost over.' The statements that 'Night was falling' (p.66), and that Elie finds it difficult to wish his father a 'happy year' (p.68), follow.

Winter arrives and the glacial wind 'lashed us like a whip' (p.77). The weather begins to signal the feelings of the prisoners and to be an indicator of their suffering. The constant references to the freezing temperatures, the never-ending snow and the icy blasts of wind highlight the brutality of the long march to Gleiwitz. The decline in temperature forms a structure upon which the narrator builds a picture of the deteriorating condition of the prisoners and their declining strength.

Style

Wiesel's stark prose documents events that illustrate the experience of fear, hatred, brutality, loyalty, despair and survival, rather than telling us what these experiences felt like. Wiesel describes events and people as they appear to him in his memory and we draw our own conclusions. Refer to the comments at the end of the discussion of the first chapter: the way Wiesel describes the departure of the train for the camps allows readers to bring their own associations and emotions to the phrases and images. Is the style a reflection of Wiesel's inability to make sense of the experience or his way of showing the inadequacy of words to convey his feelings? Remember he wrote the book nine years after the events – consider how time and distance might influence the telling of the story.

At the start of the book, the narrator briefly paints an effective picture of his happy childhood, of his family and of his community. The few details he provides are carefully chosen to introduce key information and raise issues for the reader. The reader is positioned to appreciate the integrity and spirituality of Elie's family. The importance the Jews in his town placed on religion, community and family is revealed through the order in which Wiesel introduces the characters.

Voice and mood

The main focus of the story is the destruction of Wiesel's family, his community and his people. However, Wiesel also describes the destruction of his own childhood, his innocence and his belief in God. The tone (the way his voice might sound, which communicates his mood, if he told the story in person) is quite matter of fact in most places, particularly when introducing the increasingly dangerous changes imposed upon his friends and family. For example, he states dispassionately: 'And then, one day all foreign Jews were expelled from Sighet' (p.6).

Later, Wiesel begins to adopt a more reflective and introspective (inward-looking) style through which he shares his emotions. For example, he tells us of the effect the first night in the camp has had on him for life: 'Never shall I forget those things, even were I condemned to live as long as God Himself. Never' (p.34).

Imagery of night

Wiesel uses a variety of images and symbols which are repeated throughout the book to help us visualise and make sense of the events he sketches. For example, he often notes the time of day. You will notice that some of the worst things happen at night. This backdrop conveys how the event felt and conjures up the associations that we all bring to dreams and nightmares. Darkness is used to create the atmosphere of terror that Wiesel experienced.

Night and darkness can be used to represent the unknown and the fear it holds in many ways:

- the destruction of hope
- death and the loss of all that is familiar and precious, including life
- loss of light, in the sense of being unable to see the future in any positive way
- the opposite of light is darkness and light represents God's goodness as in the light of God's goodness: 'God said "Let there be light"; and there was light' (Genesis 1), the light brought to the lives of those who believe
- loss of faith (darkness and night).

Consider all of these points to realise fully the significance of Elie's loss of faith.

CHAPTER-BY-CHAPTER ANALYSIS

Note: for simplicity, the following discussion refers to the main sections in *Night* as 'chapters', although they are not named as such in the text.

Foreword (xvii–xxi)

The short introduction by French novelist François Mauriac serves to explain what motivated Wiesel to break the silence he had kept for about nine years following the war. Having been moved by the 'trainloads of Jewish children,' likened to innocent lambs invoked in the symbolism of his Christian faith, Mauriac was horrified to learn that Wiesel was one of them.

Shame

Mauriac felt guilty when he met Wiesel, recognising the devastation that had been wrought on his religious faith and his young life, based on the differences in their beliefs and race. Indeed, it was the guilt that Mauriac felt regarding his ignorance of the treatment of the Jews, and the world's inaction when it did know, that prompted him to encourage Wiesel to tell his story so that we can learn from the horrors of the past. Readers are positioned to relate to the suffering in Wiesel's story through their connection with Elie. His story, following many others written on the same theme, comes to life and delivers the powerful message of the shame of the Holocaust in a 'different, distinct, and unique' way (p.xviii).

Wiesel's loss of faith

The personal tragedy affecting Wiesel, in addition to the loss of his family and his whole way of life, is his loss of faith and, therefore, his loss of innocence. This account of a boy who lives 'only for God ... eager to be initiated into the Kabbalah, wholly dedicated to the Almighty' (p.xix) deeply moved Mauriac. The loss of belief in one so young and so devoted to the spiritual life illustrates the degree of the tragedy of his loss.

The impact of his experiences explains Elie's disaffection with his faith. The passage of time marked by the relentless barrage of shocking events explains his change from naivety to cynicism. We observe, as did Mauriac on meeting Wiesel, 'the death of God in the soul of a child who suddenly faces absolute evil' (p.xix). What Elie saw with his fifteen-year-old eyes (the eyes that are used as symbols of state of mind and spirit in the book), stayed with him and, indeed, stays with us.

The persecution of the Jews

Mauriac sees in the young Israeli that for him God is dead, 'vanished forever into the smoke of the human holocaust demanded by the Race, the most voracious of all idols' (p.xx). Remember that the Jews have been persecuted and murdered for over two thousand years for exactly the same reason – their race. The similarities between previous persecutors of the Jews and Adolf Hitler, who established himself as the leader of the Master Race and presented himself as the saviour of the German people, are obvious to Mauriac. As a devout Christian, he was keenly aware of the dangers inherent in such false saviours. He celebrates Wiesel's survival, 'of a Lazarus risen from the dead' (p.xix), and acknowledges his own human response to the tragedy and his sense of guilt. He finally affirms his own faith in God and in the belief that man can learn from the lessons of the past. Mauriac's final reference to Zion is a reference to the State of Israel, which was established as a homeland for the Jewish people after the war in 1948. Through Zionism, Mauriac believes that 'the Jewish nation has been resurrected from among its thousands of dead. It is they who have given it new life' (p.xxi).

Pages 3–22

Summary: *This chapter introduces Elie, aged about twelve, his family and their community. Elie is a deeply religious boy preoccupied with studying the Torah and the Kabbalah. The chapter, structured around the passage of time from the end of 1941 until 1944 when Elie's family is deported to Birkenau and Auschwitz, describes the Jews' naive response to the changes forced upon them by their German oppressors.*

Moishe the Beadle

This chapter begins, interestingly, with Moishe the Beadle, a minor character in the life of the town, but a major one in Elie's life. Elie 'liked his wide, dreamy eyes' (p.3). As a structural device, this is effective because Moishe appears at important times in the story and we measure his actions and statements against our initial impressions of him. The townsfolk in Sighet are 'fond of him' (p.3) and he becomes Elie's spiritual guide.

Judaism is a religion that encourages questioning and Elie becomes involved in the interrogation of his God, with Moishe as his mentor. Their discussion about prayer and study is prophetic, especially when Moishe says: 'Man comes closer to God through the questions he asks Him ... Man asks and God replies ... The real answers, Eliezer, you will find only within yourself' (p.5). The irony is that, as a result of his experiences in Auschwitz, Elie finds that, for him, God is dead.

The bond between Elie and Moishe heightens the reader's emotional response to the events which affect Moishe: we share Elie's grief that Moishe is a foreigner and must go. When Moishe returns and tells the story of what is happening to Jews, no one, including Elie, believes him, thinking him mad. The naivety and misplaced optimism of the townsfolk, and their failure to take his warnings seriously, make the outcome more poignant.

Shlomo – Elie's father

Elie's father, Shlomo, concerns himself with the practical issues of caring for his family and community. In those days, life revolved around the town and its activities, so a good father was also a good, civic-minded man. The Jewish community are careful to look after their own affairs, and this requires the active participation of people such as Elie's father who is held in 'highest esteem; his advice on public and even private matters was frequently sought' (p.4).

Jewish responses to warning signs

At various points, Elie reports that there are warnings and gossip, but the people choose to ignore them. The chapter is littered with statements such as 'Life was normal again' (p.6), even after Moishe returns to warn that he has seen machine gunners using babies thrown into the air as targets. The Jews of Sighet have faith in the Russian army's action against Germany, and even overlook the election of a Fascist government in Hungary. It is all 'in the abstract' (p.9) to them. Even when they receive news that Jews in Budapest are living in terror, optimism prevails. They cannot believe that Hitler really means to exterminate them. Wiesel records the arrival of the German army in their streets with the cold, ironic voice that hindsight affords, as if to say 'we should have known'.

The language used to describe the German arrival is matter of fact. Not purposely trying to create terror, it allows readers to visualise and draw their own conclusions. Indeed, the word 'anguish' and descriptions of 'steel helmets and their death's-head emblem' (p.9) are juxtaposed against observations that the soldiers billeted with families are 'charming', 'polite' and 'sympathetic' (p.10). And so the Jews 'were still smiling' (p.10).

However, 'On the seventh day of Passover, the curtain finally rose: the Germans arrested the leaders of the Jewish community' (p.10).

How lives are dismantled

Wiesel documents the speed with which their lives are dismantled. First, Jews are not allowed to leave their homes for three days, then they are ordered to wear the yellow Star of David. They are not allowed to keep their valuables, they are barred from places such as restaurants and the synagogue, and a curfew is decreed. Finally, they are herded into two ghettos. Wiesel remembers that during this time his mother would 'gaze at us in silence' (p.11) and that his father tried to downplay the importance of the changes. Wiesel tells us, ironically, that his father says 'It's not lethal' to wear the yellow star (p.11). History proves the fallacy of this confidence.

The illusion that they will remain in the ghetto until the end of the war is embraced and the Jews actually feel themselves to be quite well off, living 'entirely among ourselves' (p.11), and a 'peaceful and reassuring' atmosphere prevails (p.12).

The turning point

Using imagery to unfold the decline in his fortunes, Wiesel tells us that 'Night fell' (p.12). It is, literally, night when many neighbours gather in the Wiesels' backyard to listen to Shlomo's stories, but it is also figuratively night because this is the first time that the Jews of Sighet have to confront the awful truth about what is happening to them. 'Something must have happened' (p.12) when Shlomo is called to a meeting. He finally returns to inform his friends that they are to be deported to an unknown destination, taking only a few personal belongings. Elie's mother has a 'bad feeling' (p.13) and, again, because we know what happened, her words strike a deep chord. As in a play written to create drama and tension, Wiesel recounts the failed efforts of a friendly Hungarian policeman to warn Shlomo. He also tells of an elderly neighbour, who looks at Elie with 'eyes filled with terror' (p.15).

Then begins the litany of brutality that the Jews suffer at the hands of various oppressors. First, the Hungarian police forbid them to fetch water, despite the blazing heat. We witness the joy the people experience at being moved out, believing that 'there could be no greater torment in God's hell than that of being stranded here ... under a blazing sun' (p.16). Wiesel reflects that, 'In everyone's eyes, tears and distress' (p.17).

Elie wants time to pray before they leave. He understands the significance of the unfolding events, particularly when he sees his father crying for the first time. Belongings lose all value and he describes the homes they leave as open tombs. The image of Elie's seven-year-old sister struggling with her pack epitomises their suffering.

Dehumanisation of the Jews

Wiesel documents his first feelings of hatred, directed towards the Hungarian police, the first of many who call the Jews 'lazy swine' (p.19) and who make them run when they have no more strength. He describes them as the 'first faces of hell and death' (p.19). The process of dehumanising the Jews is demonstrated through Elie's realisation that he and his fellow Jews so easily forget the people whose homes in the 'small ghetto' they now occupy. The inclination to selfishness emerges, sufficient to make them look after their immediate interests but not strong enough to make them flee. For Elie's father, the fear of leaving the known and going to Palestine or even to the village of their old servant, Martha, is too great, and he remains to await his fate. Strangely, perhaps because they refuse to be separated, the family settles and positive thoughts, with almost a holiday atmosphere, return. Wiesel scoffs at their naivety from the position of the adult looking back.

The final indignity in this chapter occurs when the Jews are confined to the synagogue and, unable to leave, have to relieve themselves in the corners of their place of worship. Eighty people are then loaded into each cattle car (at the end of the book, after their time in the concentration camps, Elie notes that the Jews are so thin that there are one hundred to a cattle car) and, despite the threat of being shot if attempting to escape, Elie says, 'all things considered, it had gone very smoothly' (p.22). However, the prolonged whistle splitting the air and wheels beginning to grind have an ominous ring. His final words 'We were on our way' (p.22) are ambiguous and not clearly endorsed by any emotion at this point.

Pages 23–8

Summary: *After the ordeal of the journey, Elie and his father arrive in Birkenau, the reception centre for Auschwitz. During the trip in the cattle car, Mrs Schächter, distraught with grief at having been separated from her husband and sons, rants about seeing flames and a furnace. On arrival at the camp, the rest of the prisoners actually see what she had prophesied.*

Mrs Schächter

Elie tells the shocking story of Mrs Schächter, who cries out all night 'Fire! I see a fire!' (p.24). The chilling description of young men holding the stricken woman down and beating her is an early indicator of the effects that their ordeal has on the prisoners. Wiesel writes 'The night seemed endless' (p.26), the image of darkness effectively conveying his feelings.

Journey and arrival at Birkenau

Elie describes the torturous conditions of their transport; the crowding, the terrible heat, thirst and hunger. Having thought that they were staying in Hungary to work at a brick factory, Wiesel reflects that 'Our eyes opened. Too late' (p.23). All remaining gold and valuables have to be handed over to the Germans in authority, and threats of being shot begin to control the group.

When they finally arrive at Auschwitz, the Jews are told they are at a good labour camp, so they give 'thanks to God' (p.27). The irony is clear. They see the flames and chimney of Mrs Schächter's premonition, and they smell the foul odour of burning flesh. Wiesel notes that, fittingly, it was 'around midnight' (p.28) when they arrived at Birkenau.

Pages 29–46

Summary: *Wiesel describes the first night in the camp. He uses the established symbols of night and darkness, extending the symbolism to refer to the experience as a nightmare. He refers often to sights that will haunt him and his fellow prisoners all their lives. Elie survives his first meeting with the infamous Dr Mengele; contrives the first of many strategies to save himself and his father; considers suicide; admits he has lost his faith in God. Elie is sent to the concentration camp at Auschwitz where he sees the sign 'Work makes you free' and is tattooed to become prisoner number A-7713 for life. Important recurring motifs are: waiting and running, night and dreaming, seeing and wishing not to see.*

The first night – surviving horror

Wiesel recalls the moment at which he walks away from his mother and little sister forever. He quickly learns to lie to look after himself, telling Dr Mengele that he is eighteen and a farmer. Mengele is described as a 'typical SS officer: a cruel, though not unintelligent, face' (p.31). He waves a baton like a conductor to decide the prisoners' fates. Like phantoms, prisoners who have been at the camp for some time come out of the shadows of the night to warn and berate Elie for his ignorance and innocence at such a late stage of the war. He tells of the young men who wish to revolt against their captors, but they are dissuaded by the old men who say they should have faith.

'Never shall I forget that night'

Elie thinks that 'All this could not be real. A nightmare perhaps ...' (p.32). The horror is conveyed through his interrogation of himself, as if he cannot accept what is happening. After seeing lorries deliver babies into a pit of flames, he wonders 'Was I still alive? Was I awake?' (p.32). Shlomo regrets that Elie could not have stayed with his mother and sister, and Elie realises that his father does not want 'to see his only son go up in flames' (p.33). Everyone, including his father, is weeping and saying Kaddish, the prayer for the dead. The first night in the camp turns Wiesel's life 'into one long night' (p.34). Using another of his recurring motifs, he describes 'those flames which consumed my faith forever' (p.34) as a sight he will never forget. The repetition of 'never' emphasises the strength of his feelings and his suffering, and helps to explain his motivation in writing the book:

> Never shall I forget that night … Never shall I forget that smoke … Never shall I forget the small faces of the children … Never shall I forget those flames … Never shall I forget that nocturnal silence … Never. (p.34)

Birkenau – the 'antechamber of hell'

The chapter details the torture in Birkenau, the 'antechamber of hell' (p.34) where prisoners are stripped, left to freeze, demoralised and beaten. The issuing of prison clothes, being disinfected with petrol, having to run from one barracks to the next, being shaved all over, sleeping standing in mud, losing shoes to brutal Kapos, being called 'leprous dogs,' his father suffering colic and being beaten by a fellow prisoner for asking for the toilet – all of these incidents explain why Elie's father's 'eyes were veiled' (p.37) and why Elie says, 'The student of Talmud, the child I was, had been consumed by the flames' (p.37).

The kind words of encouragement from a Polish Kapo, exhorting the prisoners to comradeship in order to survive, is a tiny glimmer of humanity which Elie's father has come to believe 'is not interested with us' (p.33) in the face of so much evil. And yet, after a night's sleep, morale improves, only to be dashed again with the tattooing of numbers on the prisoners' arms.

The sound of bells punctuates Elie's life and regulates his activities. Marching tunes accompany the prisoners to work and Akiba Drumer sings Hasidic melodies to keep up his spirits.

Effects on Elie

Elie lies to Stein about the welfare of his family, thinking of his own mother and sister, because he recognises the need for hope. He knows he has to remain in the group of unskilled labourers, as they are to be saved until last, but realises he should not be too strong so that he can avoid becoming a Sonder Kommando and possibly having to load his own family members into the oven, as had Bela Katz from Sighet. Survivors of the concentration camps often tell amazing stories of miraculous escapes due to a lucky, last-minute decision that even they cannot explain. They ponder whether someone was looking after them or whether it was really just luck. By the end of this chapter, Elie ceases to pray, as 'I doubted His absolute justice' (p.45). The chapter ends with their arrival at a new camp, Buna.

Pages 47–65

Summary: *This chapter details the day-to-day horror of camp life. There are flashes of humanity and friendship, but more instances of cruelty and terror.*

Key scenes

The risk the French girl takes to comfort Elie; an air raid; beatings at the hands of the irrational Kapo, Idek; public hangings including that of the Dutch *Oberkapo's pipel*, 'the sad-eyed angel' (p.64).

Elie introduces readers to the head of the tent where he is housed; he has 'An assassin's face … hands resembling a wolf's paws' (p.48). Elie suffers ongoing indignities: roll calls, marching to work to military music; fighting to keep the most basic belongings such as his shoes; bargaining to stay with his father; such terrible hunger that 'The stomach alone was measuring time' (p.52); and feigning sickness to avoid having his gold crown removed from his mouth.

Friends

In between fending off Idek's bouts of madness, and the beatings that follow, Elie befriends the Czech brothers, Tibi and Yossi, whose parents, like Elie's father, 'had not had the courage to sell everything and emigrate while there was still time' (pp.50–1). Together, they hum tunes and recite Hebrew chants. Elie reveals his shame at being angry with his father for not being able to march properly and for failing to work to Idek's standards, which result in Idek beating him. He also feels shame at wanting to avoid being beaten himself. The work in the electrical warehouse is not difficult, and the Jewish head of his block, Alphonse, tries to find soup for those who need it most. After Idek beats Elie, a French girl comforts Elie, risking her life by speaking to him in German. In a chance meeting with her after the war, he discovers that she is Jewish.

Pointless suffering

In a scene that illustrates the pointlessness of much of what happens in the camp, Elie is forced to relinquish his gold tooth to Franek, a Polish foreman. Franek grows 'kinder' but is soon transferred to another camp and Elie knows that he has lost his 'crown for nothing' (p.56). Elie also suffers senseless and cruel abuse when he finds Idek with a girl.

A man dies trying to reach the soup left out in the yard during an air raid showing the degree of hunger that the prisoners suffer.

Public hangings: 'Where is God?'

The chapter culminates in the public hangings. In the first, although Elie is 'upset ... deeply' (p.62) by the condemned man and is forced to stare at 'his extinguished eyes, the tongue hanging from his gaping mouth' (p.63), he finds himself remembering that 'on that evening, the soup tasted better than ever ...' (p.63). The degree to which Elie and his fellow prisoners care more about their next meal than the value of another's life, illustrates the level to which their experiences have reduced them.

Only the hanging of a child affects the prisoners. The slow death of the young, beloved *pipel* with the 'face of a sad angel' (p.64) causes thousands of hardened prisoners to weep. As Elie is forced to look in the face of the dying child, a prisoner asks 'Where is God now?' and a voice within Elie answers that God is dead, 'This is where – hanging here from this gallows ...' (p.65). This experience forces the prisoners to think of more than their hunger; that night, 'the soup tasted of corpses' (p.65).

Pages 66–84

Summary: *Elie tells of Rosh Hashanah, the 'last day of that cursed year' (p.66). In the darkness of the night, and situation, Elie questions himself about his faith in God. Elie and his father survive yet another challenge, a selection overseen by Mengele. Elie has a foot operation and, along with his fellow prisoners, is evacuated from the camp.*

Rosh Hashanah – Elie's response

Elie no longer believes in God, nor in the hope of a happy New Year. He accuses God and feels 'terribly alone in a world without God, without man' (p.68). He sees in his father's eyes that he, too, has been emotionally beaten. Elie eats his soup and bread on Yom Kippur, traditionally a day of fasting, as 'a symbol of rebellion, of protest against Him' (p.69).

A merciless selection

The New Year's present that the SS gives the Jews is a 'merciless selection' (p.71). Elie, Tibi and Yossi survive Dr Mengele's scrutiny, largely due to the advice the head of their block gives to 'Run as if you had the devil at your heels' and 'most important thing, don't be afraid!' (p.71).

Several days later, Elie's father is ordered to stay behind in the camp when the units go to work; his number had been noted during the selection. He gives Elie his only possessions, a pathetic inheritance of a knife and a spoon. Miraculously, he survives the 'second selection' (p.76). Akiba Drumer gives up hope and is selected; with his loss of faith, he is 'doomed from the start, offering his neck to the executioner' (p.77). Drumer asks that people say Kaddish for him, but when the time comes, they forget to do so.

Evacuation

Elie has to have a foot operation, which is performed without anaesthetic and is successful. Before his foot has time to heal, the camp is evacuated to escape the arrival of the liberating Red Army (Russian). Elie's hospital neighbour is certain that the remaining patients will be killed following the evacuation, so Elie decides to leave with the other prisoners rather than face the unknown. Prisoners are sent out in their thousands as night falls and the bleak future is symbolised by the snow that continues to fall. In a reminder of human pride and dignity, the head of the block orders the prisoners to clean the accommodation so the liberators will 'know that here lived men and not pigs' (p.84). Wiesel notes, without further comment, that two days after the evacuation, the hospital patients were 'quite simply, liberated' (p.82).

Pages 85–97

Summary: *The Germans are fleeing from the advancing Russian army; the war is coming to an end, liberation is in sight. However, Elie and his father are still to experience the most physically demanding and emotionally devastating period of their lives.*

Physical torture and endurance

Worse horrors on the road replace the horrors of the camp. Elie details the torture of the cold, the hunger, the orders to run despite the prisoners having no strength, and the lack of sleep. He describes illness and its shocking consequences, such as the fate of Zalman, who, crippled by cramp, is trampled to death by his fellow prisoners.

Elie reflects on the cruel and unfeeling self-interest that makes each man fight for his own survival, such as the Rabbi's son who tries to lose his father because he has a better chance of survival without him. Elie recognises this as one of the lowest points to which he could possibly sink, and prays to the God he no longer believes in to give him 'strength never to do what Rabbi Eliahu's son has done' (p.91). In the barracks at Gleiwitz, Elie digs his 'nails into unknown faces' (p.93) as he fights for air beneath the crush of bodies. The instinct for self-preservation is the only instinct left.

Juliek plays the violin

The poignant image of Juliek, the violinist, playing Beethoven, a final triumph for a Jew forbidden to play German music, is made even more poignant after he plays his 'farewell to an audience of dying men' (p.95) because it is his last living deed.

Elie saves Shlomo from selection

When Elie's father is selected, Elie runs over to him thereby creating confusion amongst the prisoners. In doing so, he risks his own life and he notes, dispassionately, that 'there were gunshots and some dead' (p.96).

Finally, with only bread and snow for sustenance and already skeletally thin, one hundred people cram into each carriage of another cattle train for transportation to Buchenwald.

Pages 98–103

Summary: *The nightmare continues on the train. There is no food and the many prisoners who do not survive are thrown out of the train. The journey is a constant struggle against the cold, illness, hunger and the brutality of desperate men.*

Desperation and Shlomo near death

The train stops in a deserted field and the bodies of the dead are tossed out of the carriages. Shlomo is assumed dead and is about to be thrown off the train, completely exhausted and ill, when Elie awakes from his own apathy and slaps him into consciousness.

Ten days and ten nights of travelling without food reduce the prisoners to the level of animals and they kill each other in the scramble for the bread that some German workers throw into the train as it passes their village. Meir, for example, who kills his father for a piece of bread is killed, himself, a moment later in the frenzy.

Despair

Some prisoners, such as Meir Katz who 'had reached the end' (p.102), simply give up the struggle for survival. This phrase implies the quiet battle that Meir Katz and the nameless majority fought up to this stage. Shortly before reaching their destination, the prisoners start to wail and cry. Despite having survived so much, the situation becomes emotionally overwhelming and Elie feels that the crying is 'contagious ... The death rattle of an entire convoy' (p.103). The prisoners believe they are all finally going to die, that 'All boundaries had been crossed' (p.103).

Of the one hundred people who boarded the wagon at Gleiwitz, only twelve survive the journey to Buchenwald.

Pages 104–12

Summary: *Wiesel uses the wail of sirens to denote the despair felt by the prisoners, among them his own father. Shlomo is near death. Elie abandons him, finds him again, and cares for him until his death.*

Elie's struggle to save his father

The role reversal that has become the pattern between Elie and his father reaches its peak. For his own sake, Elie simply wants to bathe and sleep, but he thinks of his father first. Shlomo begs Elie to leave him to die and Elie assumes the adult responsibility of attempting to cajole and placate his father to encourage him to continue. When this fails, he is seized with rage and screams at his father not to give in: 'Father! Get up! Right now! You will kill yourself' (p.105).

At one point, having been separated overnight, Elie wishes that he will be 'relieved of this responsibility' but he is immediately ashamed, 'ashamed of myself forever' (p.106). He hears his father calling and Elie runs to him. Shlomo is desperately ill. The doctors will do nothing for him, and the other prisoners are simply angry that he cannot keep himself and his bunk clean. Elie feels intense anger towards those whom he blames for his father's death, including those in the 'outside' world who do nothing to help: 'To strangle the doctor and the others! To set the whole world on fire! My father's murderers!' (p.109). He cannot abide the advice from the head of his block to eat his father's rations.

Shlomo's death

Wiesel records, in painful detail, the last days and hours of his father's life. His death is made all the more tragic in the light of all they have endured together and with the knowledge that peace is imminent. The reader's sympathy is elicited when Shlomo begs Elie, 'You, at least, have pity on me ...' (p.110); Wiesel, after all the battles he has fought to stay faithful to his father, states emotionally, 'Have pity on him! I, his only son ...' (p.110). In response to his father's pleas, Elie brings water, even though he knows it will worsen his father's condition and acknowledges: 'With or without water, it would be over soon anyway' (p.110).

Shlomo receives a violent blow from a Kapo when he fails to obey an order to keep quiet. Like Elie, we know that Shlomo's death is near, but we can't help hoping for a miracle. No such hope is available to Elie. Elie notes Shlomo's death on 28 January 1945 when he wakes in the morning and sees that there is someone else in his father's bunk.

Elie's reaction to Shlomo's death

Elie is unable to cry. Shlomo may have been taken to the crematory while still breathing, but Elie has no strength left for emotions. Retrospectively,

Elie's view is that he may have felt relief: 'deep inside me, if I could have searched the recesses of my feeble conscience, I might have found something like: Free at last!' (p.112).

Pages 113–15

Summary: *Elie lives only for food after his father's death. He describes himself as feeling nothing, caring about nothing. The SS announce that Buchenwald is to be 'liquidated' and evacuations begin. However, the resistance organisation in the camp acts before Elie is evacuated and the liberating army arrives.*

Liberation

The evacuation of the Buchenwald concentration camp begins with orders for the Jews to gather in the assembly place. Other prisoners warn the children in Elie's block to go back to the block to avoid being shot, thus saving them. Thousands of prisoners are deported over a period of days without provisions, which will almost certainly ensure death. After six days without any food other than grass and potato peelings, the resistance movement in the camp engages in a battle with the SS. The SS flees and Elie and the remaining prisoners are finally liberated from Buchenwald on 11 April 1945 by the Americans.

Elie unable to recognise himself

Immediately after liberation, the only thought Elie has is to eat. He survives serious food poisoning, but sees the reflection of his own corpse in the mirror. Elie's inability to recognise the image as his own expresses the changes he has undergone. He says, 'The look in his eyes as he gazed at me has never left me' (p.115).

CHARACTERS & RELATIONSHIPS

Elie

Key quotes

'Why did I pray? Strange question. Why did I live? Why did I breathe?' (p.4).

'Never shall I forget those moments that murdered my God and my soul and turned my dreams to ashes' (p.34).

The student of Talmud, the child I was, had been consumed by the flames' (p.37).

'Had I changed that much? So fast? Remorse began to gnaw at me' (p.39).

'The bread, the soup – these were my entire life. I was nothing but a body. Perhaps even less: a famished stomach' (p.52).

'I was the accuser, God the accused. My eyes had opened and I was alone, terribly alone in a world without God, without man' (p.68).

'Oh God, Master of the Universe, give me the strength never to do what Rabbi Eliahu's son has done' (p.91).

'If only I didn't find him! If only I were relieved of this responsibility, I could use all my strength to fight for my own survival, to take care only of myself ... Instantly, I felt ashamed, ashamed of myself forever' (p.106).

'I gave him what was left of my soup. But my heart was heavy. I was aware that I was doing it grudgingly. Just like Rabbi Eliahu's son, I had not passed the test' (p.107).

'From the depths of the mirror, a corpse was contemplating me. The look in his eyes as he gazed at me has never left me' (p.115).

Key point

Elie embodies the characteristics of intelligence, resilience, morality and loyalty that enable him to survive the ordeal of the Holocaust both physically and emotionally. He loses his family, his home and his religious faith, but retains his ethical character.

Innocence lost

Elie, the young boy who loses his faith and his innocence to become Elie the fifteen-year-old corpse of a man, is important as a symbol of survival. It is important to acknowledge that he survives not only physically, but with his humanity intact, indeed enriched. Wiesel focuses on his journey from being naive to being worldly-wise and cynical; the elements of his character, his home life and his relationships are all part of the jigsaw that explain why Elie behaves as he does.

The young Elie is a sensitive and deeply religious boy, weeping over the destruction of the Temple, impatient to begin studying the Kabbalah. He has a keen sense of duty and loyalty to his family and is respectful of his parents. He requests his father to go to Palestine, and is thoughtful and mature.

A survivor

As soon as Elie and his father are sent to Birkenau and then Auschwitz, his ability to think quickly and strategically becomes clear when he saves himself from selection and the flames by falsifying his age and occupation. He is strong and, despite his youth, he is able to care for his father, evident when they are running through the snow on their way to Gleiwitz. Elie says of his father, 'What would he do without me? I was his sole support' (p.87).

We witness Elie's initiation into manhood through his calm, mature responses to the atrocities he witnesses. He witnesses the fight between a father and his son for a piece of bread, and notes that when the crowd of fighting men withdraws there are 'two dead bodies next to me, the father and the son. I was sixteen' (p.102).

Elie learns to survive, quickly ceasing to be a spoiled child complaining about the soup. He is prepared to sacrifice himself for his father, deciding never to abandon the older man even when he becomes a liability. Elie refrains from making rash judgements about others and holds very high standards for himself, suffering guilt when he becomes as selfish as those he has observed. His moral and ethical values are an integral part of his character.

At times Elie seems almost heroic, larger than life in his ability to withstand and to fight, all the while struggling to maintain his values.

By the time he is liberated, Elie has become cynical about God but not about humanity. Despite the horror, he always manages to recognise the positive attributes and actions of his fellow sufferers. Elie affirms the possibility for people to behave decently: in recording the compassionate actions of a few Kapos; in recognising the risks taken by those who helped others, such as the French girl; in reflecting on the ability to rise above the situation, as did Yossi and Tibi who maintained their humour; and in describing Juliek who played music while dying. Even in acknowledging the ease with which selfishness overtakes better instincts, Wiesel provides hope – he certainly battles the temptation to be selfish but he wins. He is haunted by the images of pain and suffering that he has seen, but he does not give up.

Shlomo

Key quotes

'My father was running right and left, exhausted, consoling friends, checking with the Jewish Council just in case the order had been rescinded' (p.15).

'It was the first time I saw him cry. I had never thought it possible' (p.19).'How changed he looked! His eyes were veiled' (p.37).

'I looked up at my father's face, trying to glimpse a smile or something like it on his stricken face. But there was nothing. Not the shadow of an expression. Defeat' (p.69).

'His eyes were glazed over, his lips parched, decayed' (p.88).

Elie's father, Shlomo, is a man for whom family is a sacred duty and his community a responsibility. He is a proud man, not wishing to accept shelter from the servant Martha. He represents the trusting nature and the comfort that the Jews felt in Europe at the time, so he does not believe his German neighbours can perpetrate the crimes others are reporting. When the Jews are made to wear the yellow star, Shlomo says, 'So what? It's not lethal …' (p.11). Even when the Jews are forced to live in the ghettos,

Shlomo takes the optimistic view that they are better off living among their brothers, free from 'hate-filled stares' (p.12). This traditional role makes his reliance on Elie in the camps even more significant.

Respected in the Jewish community, Shlomo is a dutiful father for whom Elie feels respect and loyalty. Shlomo is the head of the family, an autocratic and distant man described as 'cultured', and 'rather unsentimental' (p.4), probably typical of fathers of that era in Sighet. At first, we see his important social standing as he tries to keep the hope of his community alive. In the camps, he tries to endure the hardships, often relying on his young son. However, as Shlomo is physically and emotionally destroyed by the experience he loses his air of authority and decisiveness. The role with his son is reversed as he becomes dependent on Elie. Ironically and sadly, he survives almost until liberation.

Shlomo is a less developed character than Elie; we do not gain direct insight into the emotions he battles, nor are we privy to his philosophical and personal analyses of his experiences. After some time in the camps, he is worn out and Elie sees that the enormous changes he has had to endure defeat him. He fights hard to stay alive, largely due to his son's encouragement, but is too ill to survive the final evacuation. He does not assume the heroic standing of his son, but, rather, is a more familiar portrait of suffering and defeat.

Elie's mother and sisters Hilda, Bea and Tzipora

In traditional Jewish families, the men are involved in religious matters and in the public aspects of community life, while women run the home, providing a comfortable and nurturing environment. Therefore, Elie finds it sufficient to describe his mother as being busy in her kitchen and concerned about finding a husband for Hilda. The only indications that she, too, is affected is noted in her gazing at her children, looking worried, or saying that she has a premonition of evil. His older sisters are described only in their role of helping their parents with the shop. Tzipora, an innocent seven-year-old, struggling with her backpack when they are forced out of Sighet, signals the senseless cruelty of the war.

Wiesel does, however, indicate the fondness and loyalty he feels for his mother when he reflects on having seen her for the last time.

Moishe the Beadle

Key quote

'And Moishe the Beadle, the poorest of the poor of Sighet, spoke to me for hours on end about the Kabbalah's revelations and its mysteries' (p.5).

A beadle helps in the smooth running of the synagogue services. Moishe is referred to by his title because he is really a symbol of the religion which was so much a part of the Wiesels' lives. He is in many ways a stereotype: a typical religious Jew, poor, humble, pious and wise. It is Moishe who is Elie's spiritual guide, Moishe who first warns the Jews of Sighet of the impending disaster, and Moishe who averts his eyes when the fate of the Jews becomes clear.

Friends

There are several minor characters who represent the positive aspects of humankind and, in their own ways, affirm the hope and optimism in Elie that sustains him: Martha begs the Wiesel family to hide in her village; the inspector in the Hungarian police force promises to warn the Wiesels if they are in danger; the brothers, Tibi and Yossi, share their Zionist dream with Elie and help pass time with their Hebrew chants; the French girl comforts Elie after he is beaten, despite considerable risk to herself.

Wiesel shows that there are good and bad people on both sides and that adversity can bring out the best in people. There are some Kapos who, despite being in a position of authority over the other prisoners, display compassion.

Examples

- A Polish Kapo gives the prisoners sound advice about how to use comradeship to help them survive. Elie describes these as the 'first human words' (p.41).

- The head of Elie's block advises the prisoners to avoid selection by running 'as if you had the devil at your heels!' (p.71).
- A Jewish head tries to get more soup for the children and the very weak.
- The head of the block where Elie and his dying father are housed awaiting liberation acts in a fatherly fashion, even though his advice is painful for Elie to hear. 'He placed his big, hairy hand on my shoulder and added: "Don't forget that you are in a concentration camp. In this place, it is every man for himself ... In this place, there is no such thing as father ... Each of us lives and dies alone"' (p.110). He tells Elie to eat his father's ration.

Victims

Elie survives because he does not give up; he uses every ounce of his strength to fight. That is his character. Others cannot muster the inner resources and the physical stamina to do so.

Examples

- Mrs Schächter goes mad from grief and becomes an unwitting prophet.
- Bela Katz becomes a victim of his own physical strength when he is chosen to be a Sonder-Kommando and must place the body of his father into the ovens.
- Wiesel's relative, Stein, appears to be pathetic, desperate for word of his family, but this is the only thing that keeps him going.
- Akiba Drumer, a religious Jew, whose faith keeps him alive, becomes a victim of a selection when he loses that faith; his spirit and his will to live die.
- Juliek, the violinist, has a passion for music that implies an artistic and gentle soul; his rebellion takes the form of playing the music of Beethoven, which is prohibited, in the night before his death.

- A young Polish prisoner is hanged for stealing during an air-raid.
- The beloved young *pipel* with the face of an angel is hanged for his association with the Dutch *Oberkapo*, who may have blown up a power station.
- Zalman, crippled by cramp during the run from Buna to Gleiwitz, is crushed by other fellow prisoners running for their lives. His death epitomises the senseless waste of life.
- Meir Katz, the strong man who saved Elie from being strangled on the train to Buchenwald, simply falls apart. 'He could not go on. He had reached the end' (p.102). He remains in the train on its arrival, condemned to die where he sits.

The oppressors

The strict hierarchy of position and power leads to much abuse. It can be viewed as a human instinct to wield power in such a way, in order to keep those lower down in a subservient position, largely to protect a higher status. In the concentration camps, this is taken to extremes in the cruellest ways.

Just following orders?

The Nazis appoint cruel and criminal prisoners as Kapos to do much of their dirty work, in itself a way of keeping them under control. The worst in people is illustrated in their readiness to torture their own kind for extra rations or privileges. Some readers may argue that it is reasonable to do whatever it takes to survive. The frightening thing, however, is the pleasure some Kapos seem to take in their role.

The Nazis, and more particularly the SS, are portrayed as like Dr Mengele, who used innocent prisoners in horrific medical experiments. In *Night*, the SS show no compassion and carry out their work without question.

Elie's first feelings of hatred are for the Hungarian police, the initial persecutors of his people. He then introduces us to the various human instruments of the German machine, including some of his own people –

the veteran prisoners, so worn down by their suffering that they lose their own ability for compassion; the individuals who become like animals and kill for food; and Kapos such as Idek and the foreman Franek.

Relationships: Elie and Shlomo

Key quotes

'I had no right to let myself die. What would [my father] do without me? I was his sole support' (p.87).

'He had become childlike: weak, frightened, vulnerable' (p.105).

At first, Elie and Shlomo demonstrate a traditional father-son relationship, but circumstances change the natural order and their roles are reversed. Shlomo is not a demonstrative father, but there are several indicators of his love for Elie:

- In the first camp, Shlomo tells Elie it is a shame he did not go with his mother but Elie knows that 'He did not wish to see his only son go up in flames' (p.33).
- When he thinks he is going to die, Shlomo gives Elie his only possessions, a knife and a spoon, and tries to reassure his son that 'there's still a chance' (p.74).
- When a gypsy beats Shlomo, he claims 'It doesn't hurt' (p.39) showing that his main concern is to protect Elie against feeling guilty for not defending him.
- Elie eats his bread quickly, but Shlomo saves his ration, presumably to share with the boy later. He covers his kindness by saying, 'Me, I'm not hungry' (p.44).

Family relationships

Consider the relationships between fathers and sons, and between families in general, as represented in *Night*. Elie, with his strong sense of loyalty and duty towards his father that is based on respect, is at one end of the spectrum. Elie barely mentions his mother and sisters but, in his determination not to be separated from his father, conveys a strong sense of family values. At the other end of the spectrum are relationships like that between one of the loathed *pipel* and his father; Elie 'once saw … a boy of thirteen, beat his father for not making his bed properly' (p.63). Some fathers are sustained only by news of their children and wives, such as Stein. Children like Yossi and Tibi, who have lost both parents, struggle to survive for each other. And there is the mother, Mrs Schächter, so distraught over being separated from her husband and older sons, who gains comfort from her remaining boy.

Relationships between people rest on the ability of the individual to act with integrity and decency, regardless of the circumstances. Elie's determination not to abandon his father delivers the message, perhaps understood by Jews so well because of their turbulent history, that, in the end, they only have each other.

Relationship with God

Wiesel suggests there is another very important relationship that humankind has to measure itself against: that is, a relationship with God. The expectations that are implicit in any religious teaching are tested and challenged in situations such as those Wiesel describes. Wiesel suggests that, finally, individuals must decide what is important to them. Even if God does not exist in their view, they must still be true to their own values.

Binary oppositions

Night sets up a series of relationships that are binary oppositions:

- Germans and Jews (and other 'enemies of Nazism' such as gypsies)
- Kapos and prisoners
- veterans and new inmates
- the 'outside' world and the Jews in the camps
- humanity and God
- the individual and his or her own conscience.

In many ways, *Night* documents the struggle of one party in the relationship to gain dominance over the other.

THEMES, IDEAS & VALUES

The Holocaust and loss of faith

There were many Jews in Germany who were not particularly religious, but all were persecuted by the Nazis. Australia today could be described as a more secular society than Europe was in the 1930s and 1940s. It may therefore be difficult to appreciate the important role religion played in many people's lives. Specifically the lifestyle of religious Jews was regulated entirely by the teachings of the Talmud. The word of God was a shining light to them, inspiring their lives. Imagine the devastation then of those who lost their faith.

In *Night* many are tested and some cannot maintain their religious beliefs. Shlomo says humanity has no use for them, he just wants to give up. Meir Katz virtually consigns himself to death when he is unable to find a reason to fight any longer. Akiba Drumer is selected shortly after admitting that he no longer believed. At various times, such as during the hangings, Elie reports hearing fellow prisoners ask, 'Where is God?' They would have found comfort in faith, and perhaps an explanation for the horrors they were suffering, but they were simply unable to accept any longer that God existed in the face of such extreme horror.

Wiesel's response

In recording his own experiences, Wiesel provides a first-hand account of considerable power. He shares his insights into the philosophical and metaphysical issues that arise from a phenomenon such as the Holocaust.

Wiesel has 'interrogated his God' and presents readers with a challenge to interrogate themselves in regard to such fundamental questions as 'Where was God during the Holocaust?' or 'Where was the rest of the world?'

Night is overtly a story that centres on the Jews and Jewish experience. However, Wiesel clearly suggests that there are implications for all of us in the history that he documents. He raises questions about faith and human nature. It is easy to see why his experiences lead Wiesel to abandon his passionate belief in God. Refer to earlier comments on his loss of faith and review pages 29–46, his first night in a camp, the night that changes his life in symbolic terms: on that night the light of his faith is extinguished.

Although Wiesel claims to have lost his religious belief, his humanitarian work keeps the spirit of Judaism alive. The ability of the Jewish people to endure so many centuries of persecution, culminating in the Holocaust, can be seen as testimony to the strength of Judaism itself. The Jewish people have been sustained through adversity by values of the family, by the Ten Commandments, which provide a moral and ethical platform, and by the belief in the coming of the Messiah and deliverance to the promised land. Ironically, many Jews who were assimilated and not observant before the war became more conscious of their religion and Jewish identity as a consequence of Hitler's policies of racial extermination.

Q Discuss why Elie Wiesel loses his faith in God yet still retains his will to live.

Values

Wiesel raises questions about the importance of being true to one's values: about individuality and conformity and about the relationship of individuals to the collective. He warns us not to take our civilisation and culture for granted. Do we owe a debt to the influences on us, and are we enriched by our communities? Or are we hindered by such responsibilities, only truly mature and free when we strike out alone and become independent?

Judaism says that a boy becomes a man at the age of thirteen, which is when he has a Bar Mitzvah ceremony and is eligible to take his place as a member of the religious community. This brings with it responsibilities and rewards. In taking on religious responsibilities, a young man is also expected to behave like a 'mensch', a person of integrity and sound ethics. It is possible to see Elie's initiation into real adulthood as taking place on his arrival at the concentration camps, rather than at the time of his Bar Mitzvah. Here the real test of his values and his character takes place.

Wiesel's story also raises the issue of what is worth dying for. Is it worth going to war, with the risk of killing or being killed, for filial relations, such as a responsibility to parents, elders, leaders, or one's country, or for certain beliefs? Is fighting always the best option?

Q Is it worth dying for a cause? Consider the ways in which *Night* contributes to your understanding of the issues this question raises.

Heroism

Night presents characters in various situations that test their strength and courage. The reader is in a position to evaluate their behaviour and to draw conclusions about their motivations. Often, the reasons people do things affect how we judge them.

Q How do you define heroic acts? Are there characters in this book that you would describe as heroic?

Suffering

Night describes extreme physical and emotional suffering. In addition to constant beatings and terrible extremes of temperature and starvation, the prisoners suffered the agonies of fear, the loss of all that was familiar and sacred to them, and the changes wrought in themselves to enable them to survive.

Villains or victims?

It is important to reflect on the examples of ruthlessness and brutality amongst the Jews that Elie witnesses. He notes this behaviour as an acknowledgement that some of his fellow prisoners are not as physically and emotionally strong as he is. Some might judge the Jews harshly for their behaviour; others will argue that their circumstances provide an explanation which engenders sympathy that excuses them. Psychological insights into victim mentality can be applied in this context and issues of good and evil are raised. The demarcation between good and evil is not clearly drawn in black and white. For example, consider Rabbi Eliahu's son, who purposely loses his father to enhance his own chance of survival, who might be condemned as 'evil'.

Q How do you view his actions given the context?

Likewise, the son Meir, who kills his father for a piece of bread, could be judged harshly until we acknowledge that he too is a victim of his situation. It could be argued that he also becomes a victim of the fight for food, and is killed just moments after his father dies.

Q Do Meir's actions deserve such an end?

These actions, which could be seen as aberrant, underpin the despair which tragically overtakes the Jews so close to the end of their ordeal. Wiesel writes of their struggle as a testimony to their memory. Readers might remember the initial innocence of the victims whilst acknowledging their desperate deeds.

When we read of the Jews' passivity, their weeping, wailing, betrayal of their own and their submission, some might judge the Jews as weak, pathetic and complicit in their own destruction.

Q Do you think these descriptions invite judgement, understanding, sympathy, rejection? Perhaps you see judgement as inappropriate here – the adage 'walk a mile in my shoes' may apply.

The oppressors and human nature

It is worth considering the roles of the oppressors in inflicting punishment and suffering on others.

Q Trace the acts of brutality and cruelty that are cited in *Night*. What do you learn about 'the dark side' (such as capacity for cruelty and inhumane acts) of human beings? Does *Night* offer any explanations? Do you think all people are capable of barbaric behaviour?

Loss

A major theme underpinning events in *Night* is loss. Consider all of the losses that Elie experiences such as the loss of his childhood innocence, of his security and home, of his mother and his sisters, of his faith, of his father and so on.

Q What effects do these losses have on Elie? What does Wiesel suggest in *Night* about the impact of such extreme losses on his life? Are there any positive outcomes for him? For readers?

Resilience and survival

One of the characteristics needed to survive is resilience, as Elie shows. For example, when he believes he has lost his foot, that it has 'detached from me like a wheel fallen off a car', his response is: 'Never mind. I had to accept the fact: I would have to live with only one leg' (p.92).

The will to survive is probably the greatest factor in survival. Consider the strength it takes for Elie to stay awake, regardless of his exhaustion, to avoid being thrown out of the train. Survival also means retaining a sense of humanity.

Q Which characters do you think survived at the cost of their sense of humanity?

Ultimately, the book is concerned with exploring the extremes of human behaviour. The characteristics needed to survive and to rebuild a life, and the effort to maximise whatever good can be derived from such a tragedy, are also examples of resilience.

Q What do you understand resilience to mean?

Q Do you think that resilience can be seen as a gift, a lucky accident of birth rather than a mark of superiority?

Hindsight and decisions

In *Night* characters make crucial decisions that gravely affect their lives. With hindsight they realise the mistakes they made and the suffering they might have saved themselves.

- After the evacuation, the hospital was liberated. Shortly before this, Elie decided that he and his father should leave with their fellow prisoners and the SS officers rather than risk the unknown. He chose, one could argue, to be influenced by the pessimistic attitude of his hospital companion. It was the wrong decision, contributing to his father's death.
- Shlomo decided to stay in Sighet rather than hiding with Martha or fleeing to Palestine. The whole family could have been saved but for this choice.
- It is worth considering whether you think Wiesel is apportioning blame in pointing out these errors of judgement, or whether he is simply revealing cruel facts of life.

QUESTIONS & ANSWERS

General questions

1 François Mauriac refers to the Jews' "blindness as they confronted a destiny from which they would have still had time to flee" (p.xviii). What views does Wiesel express about the Jews' passivity?

2 Even in a moral society, there exists the concept of 'the other', people not accepted into the culture. Refer to two texts to explain how non-acceptance of others may result in social separation, prejudice, discrimination, violence and even war.

3 'Wiesel's representation of characters, other than himself and his father, is simplistic and stereotyped; they are there only to help him illustrate his own strength in trying circumstances.' Do you agree?

4 'Wiesel has written this account of the camps to help him come to terms, not only with the shocking suffering he survived, but with his survival itself.' Do you agree?

Sample exam topics

5 Why is Elie so dutiful towards his father, particularly as his father is described as being "more involved with the welfare of others than with that of his own kin" (p.4)?

6 "Just like Rabbi Eliahu's son, I had not passed the test" (p.107). Elie is hard on himself when he gives his father his own soup "grudgingly". How do you judge the behaviour of various Jews throughout their ordeal?

7 Wiesel says, "The child I was, had been consumed by the flames" (p.37). How and why does Elie change in the course of events related in *Night*?

8 'Elie survives only because he keeps alive the hope of survival.' Do you agree?

9 How do images and imagery guide us to understand the plight of the Jewish people in *Night*?

10 What is the significance of the title *Night*?

11 Hindsight is the ability to know how one should have behaved after an event has happened. How does hindsight affect Elie Wiesel's account of his experiences?

12 Wiesel states in *Night* that he will never forget the scenes and experiences that 'murdered' his God. Does the text show that loss of faith means loss of hope?

13 'Adversity brings out the very best and the very worst in people.' Does *Night* show this to be true?

14 '*Night* records the extremes of inhumanity and brutality, but also shows uplifting behaviour that gives hope for humanity.' Discuss.

15 In *Night*, we see that war can be the means for the politically powerful to dominate and exterminate others. In your view, does *Night* show that war cannot be justified?

16 Wiesel's *Night* has far-reaching implications that transcend the events in Europe during WWII and the Holocaust. What can this text teach us in Australia in the 21st century?

Essay strategies

Every essay is an argument

- Make sure you think the question through – look for subtleties in meanings, define terms, and consider what the instructions require you to do.
- Organise your argument to ensure fluency, as well as thoroughness.
- Decide on textual references to support your argument.

Choosing questions

Make sure you have done some real thinking about the issues and be prepared to argue your views. In choosing questions, you should reflect on the ways in which you have engaged with the text. Did you respond to the ideas and themes, or were you more interested and involved in the emotional aspects of the book, such as how the characters felt or developed?

'Unpacking' the question and planning

- The most important stage in answering any essay question is the planning stage.
- Practise your skill of translating questions into language that is meaningful to you.
- Be careful not to self-censor! When you brainstorm, do not leave ideas out because they might not be exactly on track. Sort out what is really pertinent to your essay only when you have thought of the issues and the textual material you will use.
- How do you decide what to include? The 'unpacking' of the question should help you. Define all key words and decide on your position – do you agree completely with the stance taken in the question, or only in part?
- Often a question suggests a black and white response, for example, 'War, not the individuals who wage it, is the greatest villain in this book.' Take a little time in planning your answer to consider the subtleties involved. A good answer will examine war and what motivates humankind towards it. The conclusions you reach might be qualified.
- Plan to ensure that the essay makes sense.
    - Have you interpreted the question thoroughly? Is there more than one part to address? Define all key terms.
    - Have you answered the question fully, providing suitable content?
    - Are your ideas placed in a logical order?
    - Are connections between points and paragraphs clear?
    - Is your position clear in your introduction?
    - Have you delivered what your introduction says you will in the body of the essay?
    - Have you included enough appropriate evidence from the text to support your views?
    - Is your conclusion a general statement of what you have argued?

Structure

Introduction: Remember that you cannot introduce something until you know what it is, so do not try to write your introduction until you have worked out the thrust of your argument and how you are going to develop it. The introduction is a general statement of your beliefs – the position you wish to take on the topic – and it should include an explanation of the way in which you understand key words or concepts.

Conclusion: Your conclusion should also be a general statement that sums up what you have argued. In other words, it is a statement of the conclusions you have reached after weighing up the ideas and evidence from the text.

Analysing a sample topic

Hindsight is the ability to know how one should have behaved after an event has happened. How does hindsight affect Elie Wiesel's account of his experiences?

The first step in answering this question is to break it down into its two parts. Begin by discussing your understanding of hindsight and how it works in general, and then apply it to *Night*.

The question invites you to provide an overview of the instances where the writer has reflected on the events and brought some understanding to bear. To do this, you need to be logical and thorough, going through the text in your mind and identifying where the author is reflective. Jot down all the instances that you can and note next to them what Wiesel says happened and what he now understands should have been done if only he had known more.

The subtlety hidden in this question is that sometimes there is no option available to the prisoners; the tragedy lies in Elie's wishing there was. Furthermore, it is not only Wiesel who has hindsight, but the reader who, with the benefit of time and history, knows the significance of many of the events and actions that Wiesel describes. A good answer might acknowledge that hindsight is all very well, but in some situations it only serves to emphasise how totally powerless the people in that situation were.

Examples

- The story of Mrs Schächter is one to which readers bring present-day knowledge. The reader understands the significance of her visions as being so terrible because we know they were really true.
- The poignant image of Elie as he looks at his mother and little sister as they walked 'farther and farther away' (p.29) is made even more poignant when he shares his insight that he did not realise that it was the last time he would ever see them. If he had known, what would he have done? He probably could not have done anything. Indeed, he probably would have felt much worse than he did, and may have given up hope.
- This also opens up a discussion of the idea that blame can be attributed in part to the victims. You could address the arguments:
    - that the Jews were too passive, too trusting and too naive
    - that they were continuing a pattern of persecution
    - that those who survived enjoyed some form of superiority.
- Wiesel documents the many warnings that the Jews of Sighet ignored in their desire for life to be normal. With the wisdom that only hindsight can afford, he says that even though the Fascists were in power, 'the verdict was already out – and the Jews of Sighet were still smiling' (p.10).

Look at narrative technique

The second part of this question asks you to analyse the way the story is told. This requires you to discuss the effect of having an adult perspective on the material. What does Wiesel know as an adult that he did not know as a child? Consider whether it is the fact of being an adult that provides the understanding, or whether it is history and time. Wiesel's use of hindsight is a device to describe what he observed and to attach significance to it.

Examine examples from the text which illustrate the use of hindsight to:

- create a sense of irony
- increase the sadness and poignancy of events

- show the effects of events on characters, both physically and emotionally
- show how the adult narrator uses his position of historical distance to deliver judgements and to lead readers to formulate theirs.

Wiesel has not just recorded events and people's actions. He has formed judgements of his own behaviour, and of the behaviour of others, from the position of the retrospective narrator. The final part of your answer should examine how the introspection, reflection, analysis and judgements that Wiesel includes in *Night* change it from being merely a historical record to being an insight into the writer (and not just his subject).

Examples

- The many references Wiesel makes to people's eyes (he talks about his mother, Moishe, his father and his neighbours in general as avoiding each others' eyes and weeping) is an example of making sense of an event after it is over.
- The start of the book introduces us to Moishe the Beadle. Wiesel has chosen this as his introduction because, with hindsight, he realises the loss of faith and innocence that the war caused in him and he wishes to illustrate the decline in his spiritual life as being one of the major losses he suffered.

Further examples of hindsight

- As an adult, having the distance and the words with which to reflect on the first night in the camp, Wiesel recognises the beginning of the end of his faith and his innocence. The description, 'This is what the antechamber of hell must look like' (p.34), is his attempt as an adult to explain what he went through.
- Wiesel shares with us his first impressions of Auschwitz, that it was better than Birkenau. We know that this was not the case.
- Wiesel also reflects on his behaviour in lying to his relative, Stein. He reveals the real importance of his action only when looking back and understanding how necessary it was to keep hope alive.

- Elie's decision to keep his shoes rather than have more bread shows his strength of will. We sympathise with him even more, through the retrospective commentary of the adult author, when we learn that he is deprived of them anyway and receives nothing in return. The same happens with his gold crown. Likewise, the story of the French girl is made more moving with the knowledge, gained after the war, that she was Jewish and was taking a risk in speaking to Elie in German.
- Wiesel is introspective about his attitude to his father on various occasions and, as an adult, he admits feeling ashamed for being angry at him or for wishing to rid himself of the burden of his father.
- If Elie had known that the hospital would be liberated two days after the evacuation of the camp at Buna, he would not have decided to return to his block with his father and to be evacuated with his fellow prisoners. This is the most painful sort of hindsight, the knowledge that terrible suffering could have been avoided and his father possibly saved.

SAMPLE ANSWERS

Sample essay 1

Wiesel says, "The student of Talmud, the child I was, had been consumed by the flames" (p.37). How and why does Elie change in the course of events related in *Night*?

At the end of the war Elie could barely recognise himself, the 'corpse' in the mirror, because of what he had become, not just physically, in order to survive life in the camps. Elie had changed from an innocent, deeply religious child into a young man, but with a strong sense of morality, responsibility and a belief in mankind.

The major change that Elie underwent was his loss of faith in God. He changed from a boy 'wholly dedicated to the Almighty' who prayed to God for guidance, into a man who realised there is no master plan or logic in the world other than that which men create. Indeed, he believed that 'there could be no greater torment in God's hell than that of being stranded here'.

In losing his faith he became more aware of people's ability to make choices, rather than relying on a greater power. This change allowed Elie to discover his own strength and resilience. He was able to meet the physical and mental challenges that confronted him. He recognised, through his ordeal, his will to live and the power he had to do so. He was alone, 'without God, without man', yet his instincts forced him to struggle. He did things that were out of character and different, but he maintained his humanity which had been instilled in childhood.

Elie also experienced a change in his relationship with his father. He took on the role of parent when his father became weak and was unable to make decisions and look after himself. This was part of Elie becoming a man. He changed from a dependant into a person responsible not only for his own survival but that of his father as well. This responsibility developed in Elie compassion for those not as strong as he.

The events he witnessed exposed him to the dark side of mankind. It was the ways in which various people dealt with their circumstances that made Elie recognise the potential for good and evil we all possess. The fact that individuals such as the French girl who took risks to help him, Tibi and Yossi who kept their Zionist dream alive and a kapo who was not brutal, led Elie to his belief that people can behave decently even in adversity. He learned to recognise men's limitations but not to judge, rather to live as well as he could and create an example.

The most important and enduring change in Elie was the value system that he developed during his ordeal. He was no longer a spoilt child complaining about the soup. He became much more aware of his own motivations and behaviour. Elie developed priorities, mainly to survive but to do so humanely.

He became a man who could lie and scheme to save himself and his father as the situation demanded, but he tried not to survive at the expense of anyone else. He could not eat his father's rations and he would not abandon his father, as Rabbi Eliahu's son wished to do, to save himself. When his instinct to survive made him angry at Shlomo and think selfishly, he experienced shame and 'remorse'.

Elie lost a great deal through the war, and this changed him dramatically. He lost his home and his family, he lost his faith in God and he lost his innocence. Having seen'absolute evil', the horror that he vowed never to forget, Elie changed to never take culture and civilisation for granted anymore.

Elie changed his commitment from God to man, dedicating his life to work for and to encourage mankind to rise above their potential for evil, which he discovered in the camps, and to live humanely as he did and he believes they can.

Assessor comments

Introduction

- *The introduction suggests the subtle point that the changes in Elie were both physical and emotional. This establishes the line of argument which will be developed.*
- *This familiar reference from the text epitomises his changes.*

Body of essay

- *The topic sentence establishes the main point of the paragaph and the structure of the essay.*
- *The main point is elaborated upon and explained.*
- *Elements of Elie's character and how it was affected are detailed as part of the argument.*

Conclusion

- *This paragraph summarises the main thrust of the argument, concluding with a statement of the book's overarching idea.*

Structure

- *The essay is structured around establishing the major changes in Elie, introduced in topic sentences at the start of paragraphs.*
- *The paragraphs following provide detail and support for the assertions.*
- *The last sentence in paragraphs expresses conclusions.*

Language and style

- *Direct quotations from the text provide credibility for assertions and demonstrate a close reading.*
- *The choice of vocabulary invokes the ideas of the text, such as 'priorities', 'decency' and 'instincts'. It is a mature style but is clear and accessible.*

Sample essay 2

'*Night* shows that even in brutalising conditions people still behave humanely.' Discuss.

Elie observes the potential for both good and evil during his time in the Nazi's concentration camps. The brutality and horror that he experiences are contrasted against the selfless and decent behaviour that several people exhibit. This leads Elie to conclude that it is possible to behave humanely despite brutalising conditions, but that not all have the strength or will to do so.

In the camps people can be divided into the victims and the oppressors. It is true that there are some in both groups who are cruel and selfish, and there are some who display kindness and decency. Amongst the prisoners, some are weak and cannot cope, becoming hysterical like Mrs Schächter, becoming selfish like Rabbi Eliahu's son who tries to lose his father to save himself, and Meir who kills his father for a piece of bread. Wiesel describes those who trample their own kind with no thought other than for themselves, the gypsy prisoner who beats Shlomo and some who wail and whine, having given up even trying.

Amongst the oppressors are the cruel Dr. Mengele, whose use of prisoners in horrific experiments is renowned. Wiesel describes the tyrannical kapo, Idek and the foreman, Franek, who seem to relish their roles, and the head of his tent, with 'an assassin's face ... hands resembling a wolf's paws'. There are acts of torture and killing, such as hanging children and forcing other prisoners to watch, and ultimately, burning of people in ovens. He tells of having to fight to retain necessities such as his teeth and shoes, of being called 'leprous dogs' and of being stripped and left to freeze.

However, there are several individuals who choose to act humanely and Wiesel sees their behaviour as the model for what is possible. Not all prisoners lose their will and become selfish. He recalls the French girl who risks danger to help him. Elie understands, with hindsight, his father's attempts to help him – pretending not to be hungry so Elie would eat more, saying that he is not in pain to lessen the burden and encouraging Elie to try to escape without him. Elie sees the humanity and love in Shlomo's tears, in Tibi and Yossi's Zionist dream and Juliek's violin playing.

There is also Martha the housekeeper, the helpful Hungarian policeman and the kapo who is kind and gives advice about comradeship helping survival. The head of Elie's house tries to be helpful, advising Elie to run 'as if you had the devil at your heels' to avoid selection, another advises Elie to eat his father's rations and one head of a block tries to get more soup for the children.

Wiesel does not judge the victims who descend into selfishness harshly. This is an illustration of his own humanity. He recognises that it is because of their human limitations that some are weak and pathetic and behave badly. Wiesel acknowledges that those who steal do so not because they have lost their morality, but because if they did not they would die. Those who wail do so because of their fear and loneliness, which surely is a sign of their humanity. It is those who do not seem to be affected by the events, who even profit from the tragedy, such as the kapos who turn on their own kind to save themselves, and those who become like animals scrabbling for food and sometimes killing others, that Elie sees as having lost their humanity.

The forming of friendships, the strengthening of family relationships and the care for each other displayed by prisoners illustrate that people can behave humanely. In fact, *Night* shows that brutalising conditions often create and strengthen bonds, and can lead people to discover and fight to maintain their humanity.

Assessor comments

Introduction

- *The main contention is stated clearly, teasing out the subtleties of the topic and establishing the writer's view of what the book achieves.*

Body of essay

- *Examples support the contention and show a close reading. The assertions are made and explained in the same paragraph to produce a credible and clear argument.*
- *Humanity is a central concept and much of the essay relies on the understanding and application of this key word.*

Conclusion

- *The message of the book is stated, which is in brief the answer to the question.*

Structure

- *The structure is signposted by topic sentences at the start of paragraphs, which indicate that the discussion will be approached in a logical manner, dividing characters into groups.*
- *The assertions about types of people and their behaviour are elaborated upon in paragraphs following.*
- *The acts of brutality are detailed first to provide a contrast with the positive behaviour that Elie believes can triumph.*

Language and style

- *The interpretation of the question leads this writer to explore the term 'humanity', suggesting that the question allows for 'humane' to be extended in this way. The answer therefore shows that even poor behaviour is 'human' and Elie is compassionate.*

REFERENCES & READING

Text

Wiesel, E. 2006, *Night*, trans. M. Wiesel, Penguin, London.

Further reading

Biderman, A. 1995, *The World of My Past,* AHB Publishing, Melbourne.

Blech, B. 1999, *The Complete Idiot's Guide to Jewish History and Culture*, Macmillan Publishing, New York.

Brett, L. 2000, *Too Many Men*, Pan MacMillan, Sydney.

Elisha, R. 1983, *In Duty Bound*, Yackandandah Playscripts, Melbourne.

Epstein, H. 1988, *Children of the Holocaust*, Penguin, Harmondsworth.

Frank, O. (ed.) 1995, *The Diary of a Young Girl – Anne Frank*, Penguin, New York.
This is the definitive edition, edited by Anne's father Otto with Miriam Pressler, translated by Susan Massotty; the diary was first published in 1952 as Anne Frank – The Diary of a Young Girl. *Texts titled The Diary of Anne Frank contain commentary on the original diary.*

Keneally, T. 1982, *Schindler's Ark,* Hodder and Stoughton, Sydney.

Levi, P. 1987, *If This Is A Man & The Truce,* Abacus, Harmondsworth.

Styron, W. 1979, *Sophie's Choice,* Bantam Books, New York.

Website

www.eliewieselfoundation.org

Films

Cabaret, Director Bob Fosse, ABC Pictures International, 1972.

Into the Arms of Strangers: Stories of the Kinder Transport, Writer/Director Mark Jonathan Harris, Warner Bros., 2000.

Life Is Beautiful, Director Roberto Benigni, Miramax Pictures, 1998.

Schindler's List, Director Steven Spielberg, Universal Pictures, 1993.

The Train of Life, Writer/Director Radu Mihaileanu, 2000.

GLOSSARY

This is a list of terms that appear throughout *Night* and this guide.

Beadle – An official of the synagogue.

Kabbalah – Mystical dimensions of the Torah (see below).

Gestapo – The German State Secret Police under Hitler.

Hasidism – Strictly orthodox Jewish beliefs not adhered to by all Jews.

Holocaust – The Holocaust refers to the annihilation of more than 16 million people between 1933 and 1945 under Hitler's regime. More than 6 million Jews were killed, estimated to represent over 67% of Europe's Jews at the time. Polish, Russian and Ukrainian people as well as Romanies (gypsies), socialists, homosexuals and people Hitler declared 'defective' made up the other 10 million who died. Victims were tortured, starved, experimented on and worked to death. Thousands upon thousands were killed in the gas chambers, shot or hanged. Hitler called this 'the final solution'.

Jew – Anyone whose mother is Jewish. Hitler extended the definition to cover anyone with any Jewish parents or grandparents.

Kapo – Prisoners enlisted to take office over the rest of the prisoners. They were often criminals who were as brutal as their captors.

Nuremberg Trials – The trials of twenty-four chief Nazi war criminals from November 1945 to October 1946. There were four main charges, one of which was crimes against humanity that included mass murder of Jews and others.

Pogrom – An organised violent attack to persecute and exterminate an ethnic group.

Rabbi – Teacher who is the religious leader of a Jewish congregation.

SS Schutz-Staffel (lit. trans: protective squadron) – Established in 1925, was the Nazi elite corps. The SS carried out police duties but became feared and reviled for their brutal treatment of Jews and others in the concentration camps. The SS was condemned at the Nuremberg Trials of war criminals.

Synagogue – A meeting place which has become the place of worship for Jewish people.

Talmud – The primary source of Jewish religious law.

Torah – The Torah is the first five books of the Old Testament of Jewish history and law, which all observant Jews are expected to know well.

The Angel of Death – Nickname given by prisoners to Dr Josef Mengele (refer to the section 'Concentration Camps' for details).

The Yellow Star – Six-pointed Star of David, the symbol of Judaism, was painted by the Nazis in yellow, with the word *Jude* (German for Jew, pronounced like *Yooda*) inside it, on windows of Jewish shops. By 1941 all Jews had to wear it as a badge on their chests at all times. This was not the first time that Jews were forced to wear distinctive clothing; one of the early examples comes from the 9th century when they had to wear yellow belts.

Zionism – The support of, and belief in, the Jewish homeland, now called Israel, which was founded in 1948.

Zohar – Kabbalistic books.